NADA'S JOURNEY

NADA MULLER

BALBOA.PRESS

A DIVISION OF HAY HOUSE

Balboa Press books may be ordered through booksellers or by contacting:

Balboa Press
A Division of Hay House
1663 Liberty Drive
Bloomington, IN 47403
www.balboapress.com.au
AU TFN: 1 800 844 925 (Toll Free inside Australia)
AU Local: 0283 107 086 (+61 2 8310 7086 from outside Australia)

Print information available on the last page.

ISBN: 978-1-5043-2426-7 (sc)
ISBN: 978-1-5043-2427-4 (e)

Balboa Press rev. date: 02/17/2021

This book has been written for over eight years in between marriages, trials and life. It is about Spirit and how Spirit is in us and all around us. Just wanted to share the many stories of my evolving life and how Spirit has helped me.

S pirit has helped me my entire life. When I was little I would always sense something in the bathroom never realising it was spirit and would always hurry as I was scared. As I look back I realised I had always had the ability to feel and know how people were feeling. Often I would seek loved ones out to see if they were ok, I remember my family being at our relatives' house next door and I would run back to check on my grandma, as she wasn't able to walk far. It wasn't until much later I realised I was an Empath. Able to feel and know how others were feeling. I had always felt different and was often told I was too sensitive, but as an empath you really do feel things so much more.

When I was at school one day our scripture teacher talked about God and asked us to give ourselves over to him, I did I had always loved scripture and talking about God. My parents are great people and I had a beautiful upbringing not religious but they did believe in God. Anyway this will be touched on later.

During my 30's I had a marriage breakup it was devastating. We had been married 13 years and been together since we were 15. The signs and guidance that I received during that time and since has helped me so much. My whole world and my children's had been turned upside down.

Thankfully I had been meditating for a few years and had that to help me, also my beautiful family and friends. When you meditate you see, really see, your angels, guides your loved one that have passed over and it is life changing. A few years before my marriage breakup, my grandmother had passed. It was a very hard time she had cancer, we had gotten closer once she had moved next door to my parents.

One night as she got closer to passing my mum said she was going to stay overnight and I felt I had to be there for my mum. So my husband and two children were understanding and it was pretty tough but so worth it. She didn't pass that night and the staff at the nursing home said she's waiting for someone. We thought my grandfather her husband but he wasn't up to seeing her again, he was grieving, my mum was told you could take a photo of him to my grandmas and say he was there, mum couldn't do it, so I said I would.

It was so hard. I told her he was there, we loved her and she could go if she wanted, it was ok!

Later that night around 9 she passed. Around that time my friend had started meditating and I loved hearing about her experiences.

I remember being excited by her telling me stories and after my grandmother passed I started questioning "Why are we here" "it's not fair, I remember being so upset that t wouldn't get to see her and say "happy birthday".

That night I remember dreaming of her and in my dream we were all at her house and one by one we went into her bedroom when it was my turn I went in and she said "hello darling" so loud and clear I woke up so excited. I knew she had visited me. I woke my mum at 6 am in the morning to tell her Marney's ok.

So I started meditation, I loved it. We had a great teacher, gentle and kind. I remember feeling someone at my head one night, I peeked and no-one was there. It was my angel, I actually felt pressure on my head and knew it was real. Not long after I started I started to see my Indian guide and any beautiful angel lady Mariana. Every week I couldn't wait to go and see whom I was going to see, what guidance I would get and a calm and peace I had never experienced before.

Going through trauma and heart break, losing a husband or loved ones, going through major life change is traumatic but what saved me was the spiritual world. My guides were there giving me guidance every step of the way loving and guiding me. Showing me information through signs, them speaking to me, loving me saved me. Also my parents and friends. It was funny you know, a few of my friends went through marriage break ups around the same time and it was lovely having each other to lean on, laugh with, cry with, you would never have believed how even back then Spirit was looking after us all.

"When you listen to your heart, you are going in the right direction."

I was struggling financially. It was hard. Luckily I had been working part-time in a school canteen and loved it. The beautiful bosses changed things and let me work from day one to five. I also got a second job to give out papers on Saturday nights at cinemas, which helped. Looking back, it was a crazy time, emotions were a roller coaster, money very little but having my children, friends, family, spirit got me through it. After selling my home and purchasing a new one, Spirit got me another job to enable me to get the loan. Looking back, I was looked after everything did fall into place amongst the chaos.

After two years being on my own I kept asking and talking to spirit. I was fed up with being on my own. I remember saying to Spirit please if you bring me someone, ill love him. Just hurry it up. Anyway I had dated but to no avail. I don't fall in love easily, but two weeks after my marriage broke up, I was at a friend's house and his mate called in. He was lovely, we talked about Spiritual things, anyway it was too soon after my breakup for me. He even left a Spiritual book with his number in it.

Spirit has a divine plan yes but we also create our own reality. When you listen to your heart, you are going in the right direction. After two years of being on my own, I had been out with my girlfriend and she wanted to go to the same place the next night. I said no, I didn't know where I wanted to go, so I rang a friend and he suggested somewhere else, I hadn't been before. So we went and as I was walking to get us a drink, I heard "Nada" and I looked and thought I don't know him. Then he called my name again and he said "Andrew Steve's friend" then I remembered! We talked all night, danced and we had a lot of in common.

It felt so comfortable being with him, natural. Four months later we were married.

I was teaching meditation and loved it, I have met many beautiful souls through my work. So after my 1st marriage breakup, I was teaching meditation, I loved it and wanted to help people to change their world. Knowing we are never alone beautiful beings always guiding us.

I've have had many spiritual signs from Spirit from having the television turned on, to $10 materialising out of no-where.

I have always had a burning desire to help people. So after moving (my house was too small) I found a spiritual centre in Liverpool and I was there over 12 months teaching to one committed person, and met a few others, then I became pregnant so after I had my daughter and teaching at home I found another centre at Kearns where as I was looked after from Spirit even then leading me to kind people allowing me to teach.

My passion was found from helping people. Teaching mediation and giving readings and learning crystal healings changed my life. I am forever grateful to Sharon for teaching me meditation and opening up this world. Once you embrace your intuition and trust it, it leads you to a better life. I was happy remarried having my children with me, life was good. We wanted a child and after a lot of mixed reactions due to my age and trying for two years my baby was born, I had miscarried before her and I was so upset but figured if we were meant to we would. Being an older mum this time around thirty-nine was no different, I love and adore my children. I feel so blessed to be their mother and mothering came natural to me.

Don't get me wrong at times life was hard, but meditating and talking to my angels helped. Six months after my daughter was born I became sick it was a virus but nothing like I had had before. I remember going to take my two older kids to meet their dad and I had a feeling I would have a car accident. I didn't feel well and it took effort just to drive, but I drove carefully then sure enough at the lights a car hit me from behind. It was a bump no damage to me but his car. It was a big bump but we were protected once again and my baby was in the back seat I don't know how I drove, but I did get sicker and my Doctor told me to go to hospital. So that Christmas I was in hospital and I know I was there because I made myself sick. Literally I had been told my friends weren't trustworthy and I couldn't stop thinking about it.

I was really hurt and I know through my thoughts I made myself ill.

After being in hospital for a week, I signed myself out. They had given me too many fluids and when I went to the bathroom I looked in the mirror and I remember thinking too much fluids, my eyes were slants and when they came to put fluids in my drip, I refused. At home I got better, never allow other people to tell to what to do. Even though they had the best of intentions, they still tried to help me, it wasn't the right help. And your intuition knows it. Trust it!

Giving people guidance came natural to me not long after I started meditation, I received messages for people. Back then it wasn't like today people weren't as open.

It came as a surprise to be received so well from the person I delivered the message too.

Not only were they open they were grateful. I remember thinking they would think I was crazy or wouldn't believe but they did.

I felt honoured to be able to do this. Especially them trusting me.

So after years of teaching and naturally getting messages I decided I wanted to read for more people.

I was reading at the Kearns centre, at my homes and had a burning desire to do more. I remember writing all the information down before a client would come then elaborate on it with the help of their loved ones. Never and I say never listen to others with what you can do with your life. and I mean by your goals and dreams.

I was told in a reading when I expressed my desire to read "oh no you will do healings" well I knew I was a healer, I had been told many times and I love doing my crystal healing work.

I did a crystal healing course and honestly as long as you have the right intentions Spirit will bring the opportunity. My belief is we are all healers, psychic and if we listen to that small, still voice within we can be happy. Happiness comes from within, your answers are inside you and when you meditate you get clear, accurate guidance like no other. No one can say you're wrong after you experience what you do after mediating.

"My belief is we are all healers, psychic and if we listen to that small, still voice within we can be happy."

Many years ago I was on the computer and wanted to join a group whom talked about meditation wow what an eye opener. They hadn't experienced what I had experienced what I had and so challenged me. Ego was in operation. When ego gets in the way we aren't coming from a place of peace and calm. So after years from working from home on and off one of my friends whom had become a friend from meditation told me about a coffee shop in Campbelltown who had psychic's reading there. Well I waited about a year and decided to go. We, my daughter and grandson were sitting there having coffee when I asked Spirit for a sign "if I'm meant to ask her and give her my card give me a sign, well a tiny white feather floated in from outside all the way across the room and landed on my bag. My daughter and I couldn't believe it, so I went u and two weeks later I was working there.

I had just been grocery shopping and had not one crystal or card with me but I went and it went well. Just goes to show that when opportunity comes we have to jump.

Spirit brings the opportunities. We are all channels for Spirit and Spirit works with us and through us, allowing us to help each other.

No one gets anywhere without another.

One day I remember getting groceries and "thinking is this it". Don't get me wrong I was happy but wanted more when I say more, more emotional satisfaction. We had moved a couple of times and with each time to a better home.

You see my dream had been acres. I love the feeling of land, houses didn't really matter as long as I loved it but by that I mean it didn't have to be big, so 3 of my houses were all empty for seven months before we got them.

I always thank Spirit, but have since been told it was me manifesting, I always like to thank them.

I have always asked for help but years earlier had not allowed myself to receive. I had always given and didn't want anything back not realising I was blocking blessings. When I went through the marriage breakup I learnt to ask for help from Spirit and those around me, people also offered but I

had to let myself receive and in doing so this had made my life better. We are here to learn and grow as a soul so when we grow the most it's at the most challenging times, when we are happy not so much.

We are here to master lessons and by that it means repeating certain circumstances over and over again to we all realise we are worthy.

Years ago I would say "why is this happening to me". Now I "say what am I learning in this"

As I have learnt since working with Spirit we pick our parents before we come down and our children pick us. It's all about learning.

Acres being my dream for as long as I can remember and also having a shop. I'll tell you the story of how two houses came about as I had wanted land for so long. You cannot beat living on land. Nature all around your heaven. Anyway after having our house up for sale for 12 months and I also had been looking for months found a property on one acre it was beautiful and I had always loved Camden. the only way to describe it, is it felt like home.

But it was out of our price range so I looked further afield. It was at Belimbla Park and both my husband and children didn't want to live that far out. So I remember clearly saying to Spirit "please I don't want my dream if my family won't be happy. So anyway I remember clearly the day our house finally sold I called up about the house at Belimbla Park The real estate agent said I've got a lady looking this afternoon, so I'll wait and put your offer in.

I was feeling happy thinking this was going through as I had been waiting over 12 months when the real estate rang me that house had also been on the market for 12 months.

He said sorry she bought it. I was upset but also knew Spirit would have a plan anyway out of the blue a couple of weeks later my husband said "do you want to go to that auction?" I'm like yes ok, it was at the Camden house I thought we would go!

I had driven past it a lot visualising it and had taken my Dad there for an inspection, even though it was out of our price range. So there were quite a few people there and my husband said we were interested but didn't have a deposit bond ready.

It got passed in as the people whom bidded didn't go high enough.

So two weeks later we were up at Port Macquarie out of the blue the real estate agent rang and said come up in price a bit as the other people didn't have the money so we did and a house valued at $890000 we got for $640000.omg to say I was excited was an understatement, it was 6 mins from Camden inground pool on a gorgeous acre. I remembered being scared and my husband said "we'll grow into it", and we did.

My second marriage had been both a blessing and a curse. We were soul mates and still friends, which I am grateful in saying that he was my greatest teacher. Spirit has taught me we have to have faith, faith in Spirit, faith in yourself, faith to manifest.

For any relationship to work we have to communicate, listen and respect each other. Throughout my life, Spirit has taught me that each time and over time if we are not being treated right that person will lose us. Same goes if we are not respecting the other person. We have to have a balance, give/take for everything to work out.

If someone starts to dis-respect us by not listening, or changing their behaviour or we are not learning from each other the relationship goes.

We are Spirits having an Earth experience, we are here to grow and learn.

So if the experience isn't for our highest good it goes or changes.

As long as we are listening to our hearts and feelings we will be on track.

Once we pass a test the Universe will give you another similar circumstances to see if you reacted in a graceful manner. Don't get me wrong, we are not always meant to be graceful when dealing with a difficult person or circumstance. Sometimes I have been a firecracker, but only in situations where needed. To be kind, loving and of service is right but that doesn't mean being a door mat or putting people before you.

Spirit doesn't want you to be subservient to the point you have no self-esteem. Standing up for yourselves and others is one way of helping you to believe in yourself. There have been many times where we are in situations that challenge us and in some ways its people being mean or nasty, mistreating you or your children. Each time we speak up whether it's at work, friend's, home life we are trying to heal Speaking is healing.

You cannot possibly grow into who you are meant to be if you are people pleasing or care what people say or think about you. You can be the nicest, kindest person and if someone decides to say stuff or not like you that's it. But it doesn't matter!

You are born with a main guides and other guides both in spirit and animal guides also whom are with you sending love and light to you. One meditation my main guide Jesus showed me as we went through to each house showing people alone, sad crying all the while someone had an angel with them.

It was wonderful being shown this another time I was shown me in past lives, one was the era when Jesus walked the Earth, another as a male knight, and as a male Native Indian.

I always had a fear of the beach, I loved it but didn't like going out too far. I was shown I had lived and died in Atlantis. hence my fear.

Sometimes fears from the past live times carry over to this lifetime.

There is a book called the Akashic records which has all our previous lifetimes and our lessons we have learned. We get to see this when we pass over.

Also unlike what we are taught through religion, we are greeted by our loved ones in Spirit, our beautiful Angels and we are shown how we lived our life, whom we touched, no guilt thrown upon us surrounded by love.

My other miracle house happened after we had been in Camden for 3 years and my husband was going through changes, pretty stressful times as he had been out of work twice and it was hard six months of no main income, anyway he had decided he wanted to downsize, and have no mortgage which is great, but every time we looked at other homes new and old I didn't like them. my heart wanted to be surrounded by nature.

We had sold our home due to circumstances and I kept praying asking angels and my loved ones for help. We were getting a bit anxious, I even joked we would be living in a tent!

After going from house to house one Saturday, I felt a bit depleted went to look at the computer for the umpteenth time, wine in hand and there was a house on 5 acres in Razorback! Omg I was so excited and couldn't believe the price, location. Again it was empty! A bit rundown long grass, I ran to show my husband and we were both excited as I had been looking for 3 months and again out of nowhere was this house in our price range on 5 acres. The next morning, we left to go look at it, a car drove out in front of us and on the car it said MIRACLE. Yes, another divine sign, we loved it, I always trust my heart and feelings and I was so excited. By Wednesday the next week it was ours. My dream had come true, again my husband said we will grow into it and we did. It wasn't as big as the last house, so I decided I would get my shop as I couldn't teach meditation there I was doing reading at café le chat Campbelltown for 3 years and then as it changed hands I rented a room at meditation space.

So again I started asking and thanking Spirit, for my shop. I would buy objects for my shop and thank the Universe for it.

I remember going to look at Picton there were a few empty shops, the first I liked but was very run down, my son liked it too, then I decided on another one.

Going to and fro from real estate, council was new for me, I hadn't done this before. Now we all have dreams and we can all achieve then, only you know your heart and what it wants and also as we grow and evolve our needs change. Spiritual growth means you've outgrown your life, it can mean I don't like living here anymore, I don't like my job anymore or partner etc.

Now again we need to speak up and say how we feel, because when we do so we feel better and the people can understand and compromise or if they don't care, we leave. Once you grow, you cannot go back to whom you once were we are meant to move forward, into change as then we our soul grows again.

We are not learning if we are stagnating or nothing changes and that is why, we chose to come here to Earth. To grow. It's all lessons.

"We are all channels for Spirit and Spirit works with us and through us, allowing us to help each other."

Now here I will touch on the law of attraction. What we focus, think, speak about we attract. So if we can focus on good things yay, is great because we are manifesting our hearts desires, but if we are focusing on our fears we are attracting that. It is so important to acknowledge everything that happens to us the good or bad although Spirit doesn't say it's bad just experiences. So as we are in human form we get the 'ego' with the body please do not confuse this with self-love. Self-love is imperative for us to grow into whom we are meant to be. When we are born, we are pure, essence, just being but as we grow up whether it's our family, friends, schools and conditioning to society which can damage our self-worth and our belief in our selves.

If we were taught meditation, self-love what a different world we would live in but in reality we can live in a beautiful world no matter what if happening around us. Someone that lives in poverty and someone whom lives in abundance, same world. It is our core belief about yourself that limits you.

I remember wanting my own hair salon then a salon supplies going half way, when I was younger I got picked for softball reps but was nervous, only went once but I put it down in not believing in myself as have learnt since that opportunities come from Spirit.

Everything does, it's an Energy, we are energy and that is how we attract our lessons, also I believe somethings are meant so destiny. Like people whom you meet. Now I used to be a real worrier, I would pray all the time but I also would worry.

The moment I learnt we attract what we worry about I changed it and how I changed it was through saying and thinking affirmations. For example, and I thought I haven't enough money, I could then say cancel I am abundant, money comes easily to me anything that counteracts the negative thoughts.

If you haven't got good self-esteem, it will be hard for you to ask for help or accept help but that is one of our lessons. Knowing it is our Divine right to live in an abundant, kind world helping each other.

What Spirit has taught me is we never stop learning, we are all teachers, we are all students. Life brings the lessons and it is how we deal with the circumstances that matters, whether it's a friend being mean, not being paid right in your job or being cheated on its all lessons. So when we are dealing with difficult circumstances asking Spirit to help you, your angels and loved ones in spirit you set in motion a bond of energy to help and they answer you, they answer by a repetitive feeling, thought or outward signs for example many years ago, I had dropped my children off at school and had the thought, what am I going to do today?

And straight away I got a thought and feeling to go 40 minutes away to a park a friend has shown me years earlier. kept getting it so I thought "why not".

I love driving, with music blaring and when I goth there, I thought what a waste of time, but within seconds a girl arrived crying and I talked to her and helped for an hour. It's called synchronicity, Divine Timing. Everything happens at the right divine time.

Once you follow your intuition you find magic is real. Now too many people give their power away by trying to please others. We are here to be of service yet not a doormat, or even trying to fit in. we are meant to love and accept ourselves and once we do we find a peace, we go through life caring what people think of us, or we can choose not to care and there is Freedom in that.

I was told "what other people think of you, is none of your business" I love that and it is so TRUE.

Only Spirit/God/Divine knows your heart and intention, as you do.

Well getting back to my shop, if you know me, I love coffee, so I thought it would be good to have a spiritual coffee shop. I didn't have the money at first and was asking Spirit for help in how to do that, the next day at the café the owner said out of the blue, she put the money on her mortgage, I thought brilliant, that's what I can do after a struggle with my husband we got it!

I would love to say it was so easy but that wouldn't be true as some people were threatened by me, being in Picton.

One in particular had a psychic working from her shop and whereas when I used to go buy things in that shop I was treated like a leper. Council was the biggest hurdle Every time I tried to put my plans in, I was told a different thing. I had asked Council to come out and tell me what I needed but each time, the rules changed, they made it so hard, I was to learn that it wasn't only me, other businesses had trouble also. I had to go to my member of Parliament several times, Patricia was amazing but here was a lot game playing going on, even dishonesty now Spirit helped me, I kept asking for help and thanking then and a good friend jo was an immense help which I am forever grateful.

Funny how Spirit always gets you the information you need and you find the truth. A medium from the other shop come to me for help and inadvertently told me they said things to discredit me, not nice but I ignored it. Also I found out the owner of the other shop had a friend in council hence all the trouble and dishonesty.

After being open for six months I get a call from council saying I didn't put in a DA. He was quiet rude and said he could fine me, so

I said I would go higher as you have to understand when I asked where do I get that from, he said council. The next day I received a $2000 fine and told I wasn't to open now at this point I felt like giving up.

I love what I do, I was teaching meditation doing my reading, crystal healing and teaching mediumship, I had put in a lot of hard work and now this. I was booked out the next day so decided to still do my work. No one was going to shut me down so once again I went to Patricia (member of Parliament). On the Monday after praying to my angels, loved ones, Spirit I get a call from her saying

Nada we had a "dinner and presentation and guess whom I was seated next too?" The General Manager of the Local Council, I couldn't believe it, how Spirit works is amazing. She told him about me and he had no idea that was happening to me, even though I had emailed him several times. Later that day I got a call to have a meeting, I was happy to be finally heard. I went there with my partner, my guides, my angels, my ancestors, I had never felt so calm.

They backed down and said I can open but couldn't take the fine back. Now the moment I got the fine I kept asking Spirit to waive the fine, thank you for waiving the, fine, please can I not pay it etc.

So we wrote a letter, asking Spirit for the words and yes it got waived, I didn't have to pay it. The power of prayer, of Spirit is immense. and which brings me to intentions.

My intentions are always pure, I don't wish harm on anyone, even the people who wish harm on me. I always forgive also; I was born that way but I also learnt if you have resentment to anyone you are blocking your own good. Even when my first marriage ended, Spirit continues to help us. The mate of my ex-husband also confirmed this. He couldn't believe it when I said I wish them all the best, I did and I meant it. You see he never wanted to leave. I realized that I couldn't be with someone I didn't trust. It was heartbreaking I had been with him since I was 15 and married 13 years all up 20 years, he tried to come back so it's sad for my children but I had to be true to me. Everything happens for a reason, and I realised he hadn't been appreciated of what he had, so he lost it.

But with loss and change comes growth now our life is meant to get better not worse. So if you're listening to your heart and feelings you will always be on the right track.

I am not downplaying the devastation that followed the marriage break up. It was gut wrenching trying to pay both my mortgage and car bringing up my beautiful babies on my own was hard and I

really felt for them as we had had a happy family life, but I do know we have to talk real intimacy is saying what on your mind.

So Spirit brought him back or if I wanted or a new life and I chose the new life. It was hard but also Spirit brought me friends sand as I said they were single, what a great time to have each other through the sad, fun times we were there supporting each other. So after being single for two years and dating a couple of people, going through even more lessons, I learnt from losing some self-esteem to growing stronger and not settling. One night I remember saying to Spirit please bring me someone to love and I'll love him unconditionally. Well they did. My second husband was my soul mate, my biggest teacher, we are still friends and share a daughter. We are there for each other still we both love each other unconditionally but we have moved on from being together as once again as life will have it, he didn't appreciate what he had and I'm saying this with no judgement. I had outgrown living like that, he changed lost his way as such, and I wanted to live in peace. He has since apologised many times and I forgive him as I know it's all lessons.

So in us breaking up, I also lost my acres, which didn't bother me a lot at the time, as it was more important to live in peace and happiness, now sometimes when relationships aren't working we want someone else to fix it. But it is us whom have to change our circumstances. by speaking our truth and if nothing changes, you again have to trust yourself, feelings what to do. Our answers are inside us and the Universe will give us signs to validate us. So again after trying to save my marriage, we were married 17 years and I had tried for a long time to continue but alas I couldn't. Sometimes only fleeting you think what are people going to say but only fleeting as happiness is more important than what others think and say. I don't feel the need to relay what happened other than again a lack of respect and not honouring each other. People think it's either you leave or them but it's actually the universe working its magic, moving us forward, not staying stuck and as I said it's when we don't feel like we can continue living like that, or going to a job or being around a friend anymore that's spiritual growth.

So while I was still in my first marriage I received 3 books from different people and it really resonated with me.

"The Game of Life" Florence Schovell Shim.

I love it, even though it was written years ago, it felt right to me, also Heal your life Louise Hay I loved the connection with Disease being unhealed emotions, and that we can change and heal ourselves. I remember having a bladder infection and looking it up and it said being pissed off with a partner that is so true I was. Which leads me to the connection of our health and our emotions.

Toothache can mean, trying to make a decision, it's amazing how the Universe works and no I haven't got all the answers, I don't think anyone does, but I know Love is the answer.

Love heals all things, creates miracles, I know this because of the countless miracles that have happened to me. We each have the ability to create what we want in our world, we all have a shadow side, light/dark we all suffer but we aren't meant to become bitter or close your heart. When we nurse a hurt or go over and over what someone did to us, we are again creating that circumstances or lesson to show up. So if keep going over the same hurt, don't speak my truth and say no, I will continue to experience the same situation/issues and then it can become a tumour/growth or if I close my heart being mean, selfish I can literally close the arteries in my heart.

We have 7 main chakras energy centres in our bodies, which when we spin and open helps us with our health. Also we have hundreds in our hands which allow us to heal ourselves and others. We are energy and that's why when we are listening to our hearts and feelings, we are going in the right direction. Now Spirit will give you signs like feathers, coins, rainbows to help us keep the faith. you see faith is the secret ingredient to manifesting. If I didn't have faith in Spirit, my Angels or ancestors I wouldn't have been able to do my mediumship, well I feel actually lucky that the ancestors trusted me to be able to do this for a living. It is an honour and I am forever grateful to all my guides, ascended masters, angels' ancestors for directing the beautiful people to me.

This leads me to touch on psychic mediums, tarot readers, healers etc.

"We are Spirits having an Earth experience,
we are here to grow and learn."

After years of doing my crystal healing work, my readings and teaching mediRion I wanted to reach more people and felt needed to get more confidence in myself mainly for platform, I've never liked getting up in a crowd or being centre of attention, I was very shy, quiet growing up. So I did a one-day workshop with Ezio, went with my girlfriend enjoyed it but was so nervous when I had to share with everyone looking at me. I realise now that was my ego worrying. Then I had also met the beautiful Florence whom was so lovely, down to Earth, I felt I had known her before. She was amazing and gave me opportunities to help and read for more people. First with Psychic Fairs then PTV. I remember my first fair, I was so nervous, I meditated before I went and got a message for Julie when I went to Florence's I said who's Julie she said she at the fair, I said her mum came to me she said she had just lost her mum. So I passed on the message. I love how our loved ones want to convey their love through the ethers to show us there still around and still love us. I needed that belief in me and Florence did, and so it gave me confidence, also I was approached from

Campbelltown Council and paid to work at Airds Fair, so I could help the people who hadn't had a reading before, again Spirit working through others to help others. We cannot get anywhere in life without each other. We all need each other in the circle called life and we are never alone.

Gypsys, Angels and Coffee was born and opened in July 2016. I loved my shop, I loved the people whom supported me and come to visit. I have been working there for a year and just signed the lease for another 2 years and put a barista on when my shop was flooded. I'll never forget it, I had been working there on the Saturday and it had been pouring, I had even thought I hope it doesn't flood not thinking for one minute that it would.

On the Sunday, a dear friend called to tell me to check on my shop as Picton was flooding. Well we went straight down to be told you can't go there as it was up to our knees, so I wasn't allowed to get anything out. I couldn't sleep that night but prayed. The shop was like a destruction zone, I hadn't been through a flood before my kitchen was destroyed, cabinets turned upside down. The water had gotten nearly up to the ceiling, it left a dirt mark. I really felt bad for the people whom had lost their homes. I still had mine, what was amazing was that all my crystals that I do crystal healing with all were stuck in mud under a mat, my two big beautiful angels were untouched not one scratch, even though they were upside down. Beautiful Jo, beat me there and my family came to help I am forever grateful to my beautiful kids, they are always there for me when I need them. Spirit knew I treasured those items and protected them.

So once again I went back to the Meditation Space to rent a room am lucky to have met Susanne, and Jess, Rene a few beautiful souls all doing their best to heal the world and its people. We are all one, we cannot hurt one thing without it coming back and hurting us. Which is why our intentions being the very thing that matters, because if t am speaking up or changing my life and my intentions aren't to hurt anyone that is what matters, sometimes people do get hurt with what we do or say but if our intention isn't to hurt then Spirit know it's us being true to ourselves.

I only missed one week of doing readings, and so I think Spirit moved me on to help even more people and to also deal with my marriage as it wasn't great at the time. And so it is. When Florence called and said do you want to go on PTV I was excited but scared, but before I could go on it the show was cancelled. But again when it came back she asked me again and said now or never. I jumped again first feeling was excitement and then fear, I was scared but my daughter said mum it's so you can help more people. My fear being in front of a crowd was being faced because my daughter was right. Even though I can teach this, I know Spirit was answering my dream of helping more people, never did this idea occur to me. I'll never forget the first night Florence was amazing and I remember my knees were knocking with nervousness but I remember my guides, Angels, ancestors wouldn't let me down. See they won't bring an opportunity then let you fall. I was out of my comfort zone having to read with people watching, but having no one in front to validate you, also it was through picture message, or text, voice message. It's easier with the vibration, of text or voice, but because everything is energy absolutely you can pick up on items, jewellery, photos.

I loved it, I loved helping people to connect with their family in spirit, some people were suicidal, felt isolated didn't have anyone to help them and I loved helping them to know also that I they are not alone ever 'there is life after death. I met some beautiful, like minded souls there too, not only other readers, the crew Elliot, Ryan and Matt beautiful people.

At different times in our life, we feel we have no one there, sometimes even if you have family or friends they are going through their own things so it is good to remember you have your Angels, guides and loved ones in Spirit helping you, guiding, you, loving you.

"Sometimes fears from the past live
times carry over to this lifetime."

I want to share with you about an incident that happened at my shop in Picton.

It was just after my meditation class had finished and I was making coffee for me and my friend.

When one of the ladies Tammy messaged me asking were we alright, there's been a shooting and you're in lockdown. Well we didn't know, so as we looked outside police were there and we were told to get inside and don't come out. until we are told too.

So while we were on internet finding out stuff, we learnt that there was a shooting at shell service station.

Anyway while were debating my friend said he will get shot by police, but I kept getting he will suicide.

We could hear the police out the back of my shop and I decided to make another coffee, the spirit of the deceased, that had been shot came to me frantic he was asking me to save his friend. I'll never forget it I was pacing up and down and friend said what's wrong and I told her. I said to the man, I can't go out there, I don't know what

I can do, and so I'll pray and ask for help from angels He went and sadly his mate shot himself

They were friends whom had an argument whilst walking to the petrol station, something happened to make one snap and kill his friend, what is amazing is how, he thought of nothing of himself, only to save the mate that had just shot him. As soon as we are soul we remember why we came down and only love matters. I am a believer that we can't go before our time.

That's why we hear things like I nearly died, I should have died it wasn't there time. Whatever your religious beliefs are can assure you everyone goes to heaven. We are greeted with so much love and support, never judgement. My mother told me I nearly died, when I was a baby they put me in an oxygen tent and said she's in Gods hand now. Luckily I survived. Even when we feel we can't go on anymore and I am sure we all feel this way at times, it's to actually make us stronger, to find the strength in your heart, to keep lovely unconditionally, to be love.

I remember doing a reading and the lady said I hate my job but I have to stay there, I want to move but my son wants to buy a house but he hasn't the money yet and finally her boyfriend said he would let her know if he wants a commitment by October. Well no wonder she was feeling stuck and desperately unhappy. Her mum's spirit said, leave your job, look for something else, put your house on the market and sell it, tell your boyfriend if you don't want a commitment now see you later.

That was a classic example with how people give their power away.

"Love heals all things, creates miracles, I know this because of the countless miracles that have happened to me."

We are meant to be kind, loving but not putting what others needs before ourselves. Spirit will always have your back. as long as your intentions are pure. One night I was teaching meditation at my house and after everyone left, I made my husband and I a milo and as soon as I got to the bedroom and put our milos down A bat appeared in the room, flying around and around the ceiling. My husband yelled and I stood in amazement as I opened our veranda door, it flew around for several minutes, as we waited for it to go. I knew Bat meant initiation and I knew it was a big sign from Spirit so a week later again teaching mediation, a new person same as well, I was relaying the story about what had happened and I knew someone thought I was lying, next minute we had a bat flying in the lounge room oh my god women screaming everywhere as I yelled out to Andrew, he came running with nets from the pool and caught the bat. The new lady never came back!

But I knew Spirit was letting them know, I was telling the truth. Later on at Camden Show, I had a reading with Florence she said have you got birds flying around in your house. I said Bats We laughed and she indeed validated that it was a sign from Spirit.

When you are in sync with Spirit magic happens.

Another time I went to see my Aunty in hospital and didn't like the food there, so I thought I'll get her maccas for breakfast, so I ordered her food and a coffee each. After they told me to wait I was thinking "gee, I feel like a hash brown" why didn't I get myself one.

After a while I thought gee I've been waiting a long time, the girl came out handed me the food and said "sorry for the long wait here's a free hash brown. Well I smiled and looked up and said Thank you!

What I have learnt is that I have been manifesting. It always gives credit to Spirit, my angels and guides but they told me it's you manifesting, give yourself credit. But I always, always give thanks for my blessings.

Following your intuition, is magic, pure magic there are many examples I can give you but a few come to mind. like asking your angels, Spirit to help you for example one day I had my daughter and grandkids in the car and I had to go to the bank so I asked my angels for a carpark outside the bank and I kept thanking them. As I pulled up a traffic lights, three people went to their cars one, after one and drove up leaving me to just drive right up in front of the bank. I had the biggest smile on my face like I said magic.

Sometimes I have had people ring running late whilst I also was running late, Spirit at work again. So I didn't make them have to wait. If you see the number 444 it means your angels are with you and I can't tell you how many time I've needed to see that, when my 2nd marriage was breaking up I was having a pretty rough day feeling fragile and I had to go and buy incense and candles at the shop which was a 10-minute walk and back, just as I got to back my room my foot started hurting me I thought that's weird as it hadn't hurt at all walking anyway „ I sat on the floor, took my boot off and there was an angel wings brooch. I cried, there way of saying "we've got you!

My Grandfather died at 94, we were pretty lucky to have him that long and he was such a beautiful, strong, humorous man.

He spent the last 5/6 months of his life in hospital.

I had a psychic party to go to that Sunday my dear friend Louise had arranged it and I kept thinking I won't do it. He will pass Sunday.

At 7.30 am my mum rang me and told me had passed earlier that morning I raced over to her and later that day I was mopping and crying and I heard Hey sis, my grandpa called everyone sis. I was so happy, he had come to see me and tell me he had made it to the light.

You see years earlier; I was guided by Spirit to tell him to go to the light when you die. I remember thinking how am I going to say that, how am I going to bring death up as he believed when you die that it, nothing else. Anyway after teaching meditation I drove to his house, was saying hello and my mum walked into the kitchen and said something about dying, I couldn't believe it so I said you know Farvey you go to the light when you die.

Amazing how Spirit works. As you follow and trust your intuition, trust Spirit and your guides you go up in levels of evolution.

When I look back to the information I was given in my readings to now, it has changed. The more Spirit trusts you, the more you are shown. You are a channel for Spirit. We all are.

Every time when I look back on my life Spirit has been looking after me. We are in interesting times, so called "coronavirus."

From the moment this virus was talked about on the news, I felt deeply it wasn't authentic.

Every time I heard a new rule, my heart sank and I felt angry. I felt down to my bones that something wasn't right. Even though I never watched the news, I love listening to music and as I was making my coffee the new came on saying "Richard Wilkins has coronavirus. They were interviewing him as they said when you felt sick as he replied "I don't even feel sick

That was a validation, Spirit had me in the right place to hear this, my feelings and intuition talk to me and I have listened and trusted them for years, I wasn't about to discount it now.

As the news became more fear based every day I decided to visit my parents to reassure them, telling them it's not as bad as the news and ads are telling you. To bring peace and calm, to make people feel better is what I do and whom I am, as we were driving back home from my parents, and I was talking about the Corona virus, I saw a sticker on a car saying "FAKE". Another time I happened to see the news on TV and it's just so happened that they had a passenger whom was being interviewed on TV from a hospital bed. He said everyone got tested as they left the ship and we had been told he had tested positive. After getting a headache, he thought he'd better go to hospital and he didn't look sick, said he had chills, fever and they would be letting home in the morning, again validation from Spirit, n that we are being sold a fabrication.

As I have been doing readings Spirit has had been telling me to calm people and their loved ones also have been reassuring everyone not to fear, to go outside in nature, play music to keep our vibration high. The opposite to what the news, media have been saying. We are being bombarded by the media and radio, we are in a fight against light and dark. Spirit we are, God in in us and we are in God.

We are limitless and at this time we are mother Earth is being enveloped with love, raising our vibration going into 5th dimension where we will all be manifesting instantly what we are thinking at this moment more than ever it is important to be in nature, sunlight, playing music, meditating so we can raise our vibration and have inner peace.

Spirit has been helping me with fellow light workers, sending me videos of the truth of what is happening. Allot of people are listening to the news and fear based thoughts rather than trusting their own intuition and feelings.

It's a fine line with wanting to tell people what's going on and not wanting to scare them. But truth be known, we are in a time of enlightenment, the time has come for humanity to wake up to the fact we can all live in peace, love and be there for each other. Rather than living in a materialist, debt driven, ego based mentality. We are all Spirit, we are all equal, we all make a difference by shining our light out into the Universe. Every one of us make a difference and we can all live and learn together, not living in fear. They want me to speak of the betrayals I have had in my life and there have been a few.

Now if people do not love themselves they will project their insecurities onto us and talk about us behind our back, but it doesn't matter as I've said before it doesn't matter what others think say about you, it's a reflection of them. We are all born pure little souls, without an ounce of pretension we are whom we are, until we become influenced by the people in our family, society, jobs, school, relationships etc.

This is where the emotional blocks can form, when we don't deal with what has hurt or happened to us, we can keep going through the same situations, and leading to a frustration and depression as we are not getting the lesson.

As we grow and learn and speak our truth our self-esteem rise bringing new and better experiences for us. Now no one is better than anyone else but better behaved and as we realise we don't have to put up with certain behaviours from others, we attract more like minded people.

When we are born, we are perfect little beings, just being ourselves, our parents or the main caretaker is our role model and we copy them. From the time we are born we are influenced by our families, school, friends, siblings etc. and some are mean. Now when I say this I'm not judging it's an observation, hurt people hurt people. The kids that bully or say mean things feel insecure or haven't enough self-love, in other words they're hurting. Imagine if we were taught self-love in school, or meditation? What a wonderful world it would be. We are living an illusion; this Earth experience is school. Let's face it school most time isn't a great experience for a lot of us. We are taught things that don't really help us and also as you awaken you find the truth that we are taught at school isn't the truth alas I'm not going to go in-depth in that as I want you to know when you look at life as it is, a human experience, you can try not to take a lot of things personally.

In saying that I'm not undermining how hard this human experience can be but we are here to learn and our soul grows within the challenging time.

"We cannot get anywhere in life without each other. We all need each other in the circle called life and we are never alone."

As beings of energy we have seven main energy centres called Chakras they are openings for life energy to flow into and out of our aura.

Their function is to visualise the physical body and to bring about the development of our consciousness. They are associated with our physical, mental and emotional interactions.

Red base/root chakra

represent our foundation and feeling of being grounded.

Location Base of spine tail bone area

Emotional issues = survival issues such as financial independence, money food.

Orange sacral/naval chakra

Our connection and ability to accept others and new experiences.

Location lower abdomen 2 inches lower than belly button

Emotional issues-sense of abundance, wellbeing, pleasure, sexuality

Yellow solar plexus chakra Our ability to be confident and in control of our lives Location stomach area.

Emotional issues self-worth, self-confidence, self esteem

Pink/green HEART chakra

Our ability to love.

Location Centre of Chest, just above heart.

Emotional issues love, joy, inner peace.

Blue Throat chakra

Our ability to communicate

Location throat Emotional issues. Communication, self-expression of feelings, truth

Purple Third Eye chakra

Our ability to focus on and see the big picture

Location forehead, between the eyes

Emotional issues intuition, imagination, wisdom, ability to make decisions

White / purple white crown chakra

The highest Chakra represents our ability to receive.

Location crown/top of head

Emotional issues universal peace, seeing connections in all things.

Blockages in Chakras

Blockage of the Root Chakra

Manifests itself as fears, anxiety disorders and even nightmares. If the blockage manifests physically it is usually through problems with the bladder, lower back, feet or legs.

Blockage of the sacral/naval chakra

Manifests through general emotional instability or through feeling creatively uninspired, fearing change, feeling depressed or indulging in addiction like behaviours. Physical manifestations of sacral chakra misalignment include sexual dysfunction.

Blockage of the solar plexus chakra

You will experience symptoms of difficulty making decisions, low self-esteem or control, anger issues. You can procrastinate, let others take advantage of you easily. Physical manifestations include digestive issues, tummy aches or problems with gas.

Blockage of heart chakra

Will opens doors to emotions such as jealousy, anger, fear of betrayal grief, and hatred towards others and yourself. It common manifestation is through holding grudges against someone or something.

When one holds onto hurt it nurtures their negative feelings cutting them off to achieve inner peace.

Physical manifestation can be hardened arteries, heart issues.

Blockage of the throat chakra

manifest in peculiar ways. Affected person will have trouble speaking up, will find it difficult to remain focused and pay attention and with often fear being judged by others. These manifestations can hinder their ability to see clearly and see things as they really are.

Physical manifestation of blockage can be sore throat, issues with thyroid gland, shoulder and neck stiffness and headaches.

Blockage of third eye chakra

Manifest as trouble to trust your inner voice and access your intuition to remember important facts or learn new skills.

Some of the physical manifestations of blockage of third eye are headaches, dizziness and issues with brain health. Anxiety, depression and judgmental behaviour.

Blockage of crown chakra

If your crown chakra is blocked you can experience feelings of emotional distress, isolation and disconnection from other people and events. You can open your crown chakra through meditation and yogic exercises.

The reward will be moments of Spiritual connection and inner peace.

When I am doing my readings/crystal healings or teaching meditation I am channeling information, from higher realms we are all channels we are all one. We cannot hurt anything or anyone on purpose without it coming back to our selves.

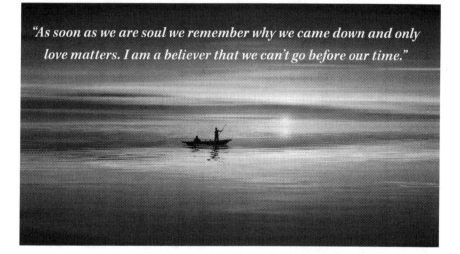

"As soon as we are soul we remember why we came down and only love matters. I am a believer that we can't go before our time."

When you spin and visualise a crystal in your chakras, you are actually balancing them. yes, go to a healer like me or also learn that we all have the ability to heal ourselves.

Crystals have amazing qualities which actually heal us. they act as conductor's amplifiers and purifiers that transmit and transform our energy in line with their unique set of qualities.

They can clear us of energies that no longer serve us and realign our energy to be in harmony with our soul to restore well, vitality and the expression of our higher gifts.

Using crystals is about working with life force to bring through what we are. There are thousands of crystals but here are a few basic ones

CLEAR QUARTZ — master healers will amplify energy.

AMETHYST — awakener of third eye, calming tranquility

AGATE — warrior stone, enhances courage and strength

AMAZONITE — inspiration, communication

ADVENTURINE — strong healing energy, balances emotions

CARNELIAN — enhances creativity, recycles past life, speeds up karma

CITRINE — stone of success, money, prosperity, raises self esteem

FLUORITE — helps memory, wisdom

JASPER — said to be helpful for controlling the emotions

ROSE QUARTZ — know for the love stone aids in peacefulness, calm in relationships, said to ease stress and tension. Help steep.

When we are going through challenging times our soul is growing and sometimes we will outgrow our homes, jobs, friends, partners. As I said previously if we ignore our feelings and continue to live the same life, we can become depressed, leading to health issues. If we are speaking our truth, saying how we feel and following and trusting our intuition we will align with our wishes. Feeling happier and our vibration will lift and we can have, vibrant health.

Meditation heals your mind, body and soul, as you connect with your guides, ancestors, angels you are shown past lives, information about people and circumstances to help you. You also feel a peace as you are reminded you never die, you are being guided by higher beings, we are having an Earth experience. Well I hope this book helps those whom wish to develop their self-esteem their psychic senses.

Nada Muller

I continue to work doing my crystal healings, psychic mediumship readings and classes teaching meditation and I love it all. I love working for Spirit and meeting beautiful souls. Thank you, I am so grateful you took the time to read my story love to you all.

"Spirit will always have your back. as long as your intentions are pure."

AFFIRMATIONS

I love and accept myself.

I am worthy of the greatest life and love.

What I am seeking is now seeking me.

Money comes easily to me.

Everything and everyone prospers me now.

I am abundant and debt free.

"Every one of us make a difference and we can all live and learn together, not living in fear."

NOTES

NOTES

NOTES

NOTES

Printed in the United States
By Bookmasters